THE HISTORY OF JUNETEENTH

A History Book for New Readers

Written by
Arlisha Norwood, PhD

Illustrated by
Sawyer Cloud

ROCKRIDGE PRESS

To my hope and joy: my family
Special thanks to the
History Consultants

First Rockridge Press trade paperback edition May 2022

For general information on our other products and services, please contact our Customer Care Department within the United States at (866) 744-2665, or outside the United States at (510) 253-0500.

Hardcover ISBN: 979-8-88608-676-8 | Paperback ISBN: 978-1-68539-441-7 | eBook ISBN: 978-1-68539-811-8

Manufactured in the United States of America

Series Designer: Angela Navarra
Interior and Cover Designer: Jane Archer
Art Producer: Hannah Dickerson
Editor: Eliza Kirby
Production Editor: Melissa Edeburn
Production Manager: Martin Worthington

Illustrations © 2022 Sawyer Cloud. Photography © Niday Picture Library/Alamy Stock Photo, p. 50; William Warren/Alamy Stock Photo, p. 52; Richard Levine/Alamy Stock Photo, p. 53. All maps used under license from Creative Market.

Author photo courtesy of Jason A. Alston

10 9 8 7 6 5 4 3 2 1

Printed in China

CONTENTS

CHAPTER 1

SETTING THE STAGE

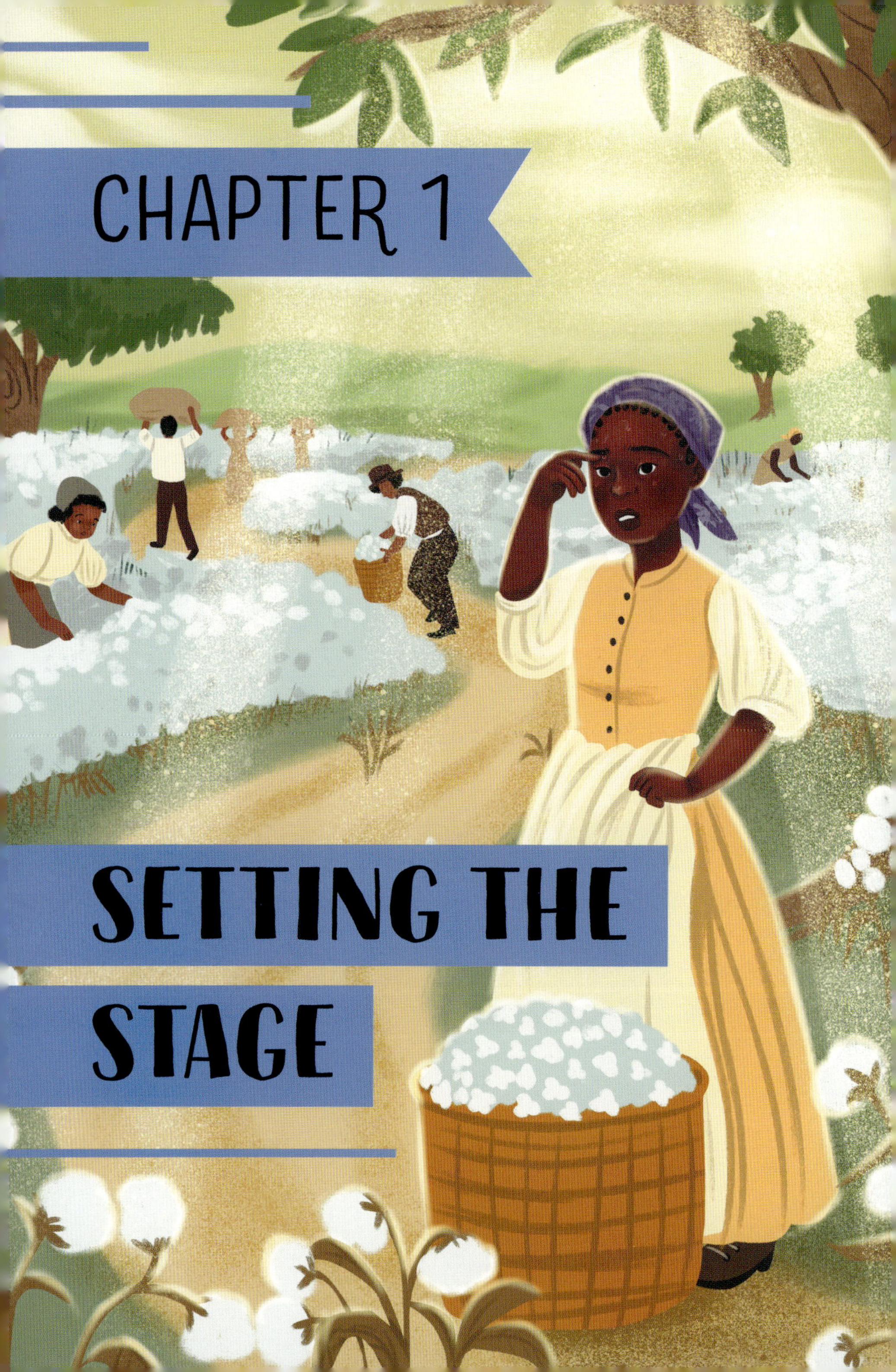

Understanding Juneteenth

When Sarah Ashley was a child, she thought about a life different from her own. She imagined playing outside and laughing with her friends. She dreamed about freedom. She wanted to be an ordinary kid.

Unfortunately, she could not. Sarah Ashley was born **enslaved**. She was forced to work under harsh and dangerous conditions. She was considered the property of another person. She was bought and sold without her permission, as if she were an item in a store. Sarah's entire family had been sold, too. They were separated and sent to other places. She knew that slavery was evil. She knew she was supposed to be free. Instead of thinking about the awful and scary work, she dreamed of the day that everything would change.

On June 19th, 1865, Sarah encountered her "burst of freedom."

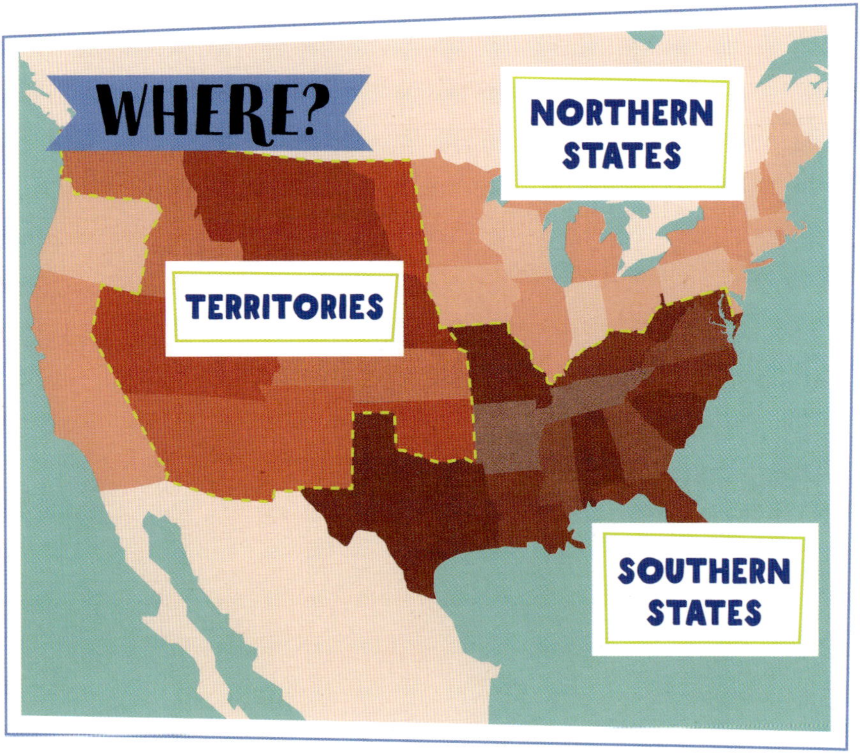

This book is about Sarah Ashley's journey from slavery to a new world of dreams. It is also about the history of a holiday called Juneteenth, a celebration of that journey. Although this story is full of determination and courage, many of the chapters will teach about the difficulties that Sarah and other African Americans faced.

At times, while reading, you may feel discouraged.

But I invite you to think like Sarah: Dream! And focus on freedom! By doing so, you will be inspired to keep trying no matter what obstacles you may face. And by the end, you'll have all the joy you need to celebrate Juneteenth. I hope you are encouraged to imagine and create a new world, just like Sarah Ashley.

JUMP IN THE THINK TANK

What are some other important holidays in history? How do you celebrate those holidays?

Slavery in America

Hundreds of years ago, people throughout the world traveled to the **continent** of Africa. Africa was a very rich continent. Several West African countries had large cities. Many Africans were wealthy and successful.

White people from Europe did not see Africans as equals. They believed people who were not European were **inferior**. These **racist** ideas became very popular. Europeans captured and enslaved Africans. Europeans used slavery throughout the world. When they colonized America, they brought slavery with them.

By 1804, slavery was illegal in the Northern United States. In the Southern states, it was still allowed. Many Southern farms were big **plantations** that needed a lot of labor to make money. Southern farmers did not pay enslaved people. They made even more money this way.

Enslaved Africans were forced to work every day. Enslavers viewed them as property, not as people. Enslaved people faced violence from enslavers. They could also be sold to other enslavers at any time. Families could be separated, like Sarah's was.

Enslaved people fought back. Some ran away or refused to work. They even formed an **Underground Railroad** that secretly helped enslaved people escape to the Northern states.

WHO?

Harriet Tubman escaped slavery in Maryland in 1849. She returned to the South to help more than 70 enslaved people to freedom. Later she was a spy in the Civil War!

In order to stop enslaved people from escaping, the United States **Congress** passed laws called the Fugitive Slave Acts. These laws said anyone who escaped slavery had to be returned to their enslavers. One law even allowed Southerners to travel to the North to capture free Black people and bring them back to slavery. This law meant that even if enslaved people made it to the North, they were never free.

WHEN?

1619 — Enslaved Africans arrive in America.

1793 — The first Fugitive Slave Act is passed.

1804 — Slavery is illegal in the Northern states.

1850 — The second Fugitive Slave Act is passed.

CHAPTER 2

THE CIVIL WAR

The North vs. the South

After Northern states **abolished** slavery, life for Black people in the North got better. They could be paid for their work and even go to school. In Southern states, Black people still were not free. They could not work for themselves or move about freely. Learning to read was also illegal. If Black people tried to leave plantations, they faced violence.

Soon the country started to expand west. As new states and **territories** became part of America, Northern and Southern states began to clash. Would the new territories be allowed to use enslaved labor? And, more important, who would decide whether a territory became a slave state or a free state?

In 1854, politicians decided to add Kansas and Nebraska to the United States. Southerners wanted these territories to become slave states.

JUMP IN THE THINK TANK

Why did enslavers fight to spread slavery? Why did others fight against the spread of slavery?

They did not want the free states to outnumber them. The North argued that Kansas and Nebraska should be free states.

By 1860, the country was in trouble. At the end of the year, a new president, Abraham Lincoln, was elected. He was against the spread of slavery. Enslavers in Southern states decided they no longer wanted to be a part of the United States. They **seceded** and created a new constitution. They even elected their own president! They called the country the Confederate States of America. The Northern states were known as the **Union**.

WHO?

Abraham Lincoln became president in 1861. He used his first speech to ask Southerners to stay in the Union. One month later, however, the war began.

The Southern states were called the **Confederacy**. The split led to the Civil War.

The Fight for Freedom

On April 12, 1861, the Civil War broke out at Fort Sumter in South Carolina. The Union lost the first battle. President Lincoln was worried, so he increased the number of Union troops.

The Union Army was larger, but most of the war was fought in the South. The Confederate troops knew the land better than the Union soldiers.

The armies next faced off at the Battle of Bull Run in Virginia. The Confederate Army won this battle, too. At the next fight, the Battle of Shiloh in Tennessee, the Union won. Many soldiers were injured or died. The Union win did not feel like a victory.

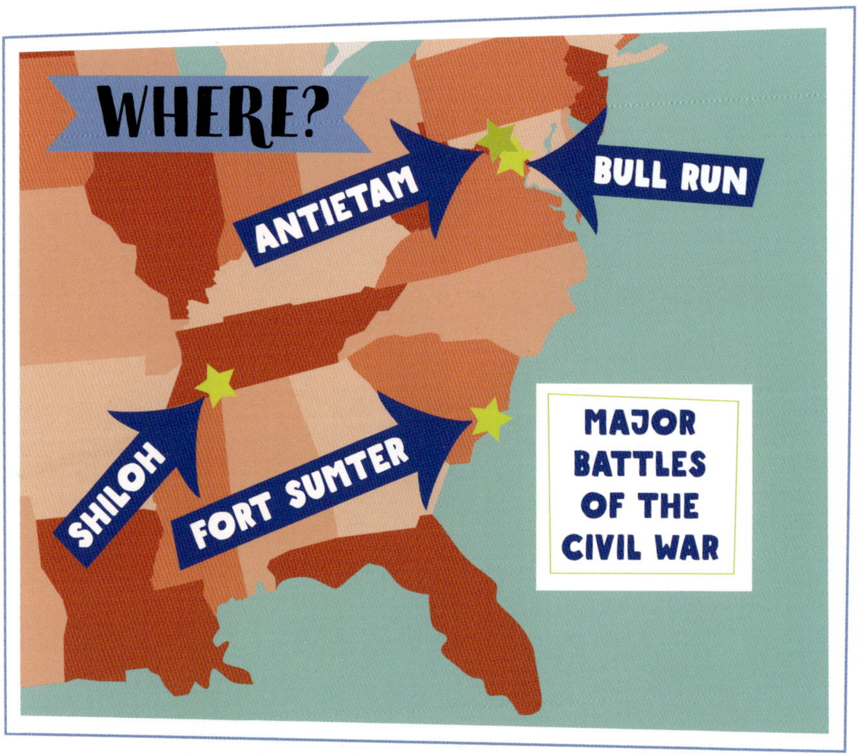

Throughout the war, many Southerners continued to use enslaved Black people to work their farms. Enslaved people also worked in factories to make the materials the Confederacy needed to fight the war. As fighting continued in the South, many homes and entire towns were destroyed.

When the Civil War started, many Americans believed it would last only a few months and the North would easily win. They were wrong. The Civil War turned out to be long and deadly. Union and Confederate soldiers faced hardship.

WHEN?

Abraham Lincoln is elected president.

NOVEMBER 6, 1860

The Confederate States create a constitution.

FEBRUARY 1861

The Civil War begins.

APRIL 12, 1861

The Battle of Bull Run is fought.

JULY 21, 1861

The Battle of Shiloh is fought.

APRIL 6–7, 1862

The Battle of Antietam is fought.

SEPTEMBER 17, 1862

CHAPTER 3

THE EMANCIPATION PROCLAMATION

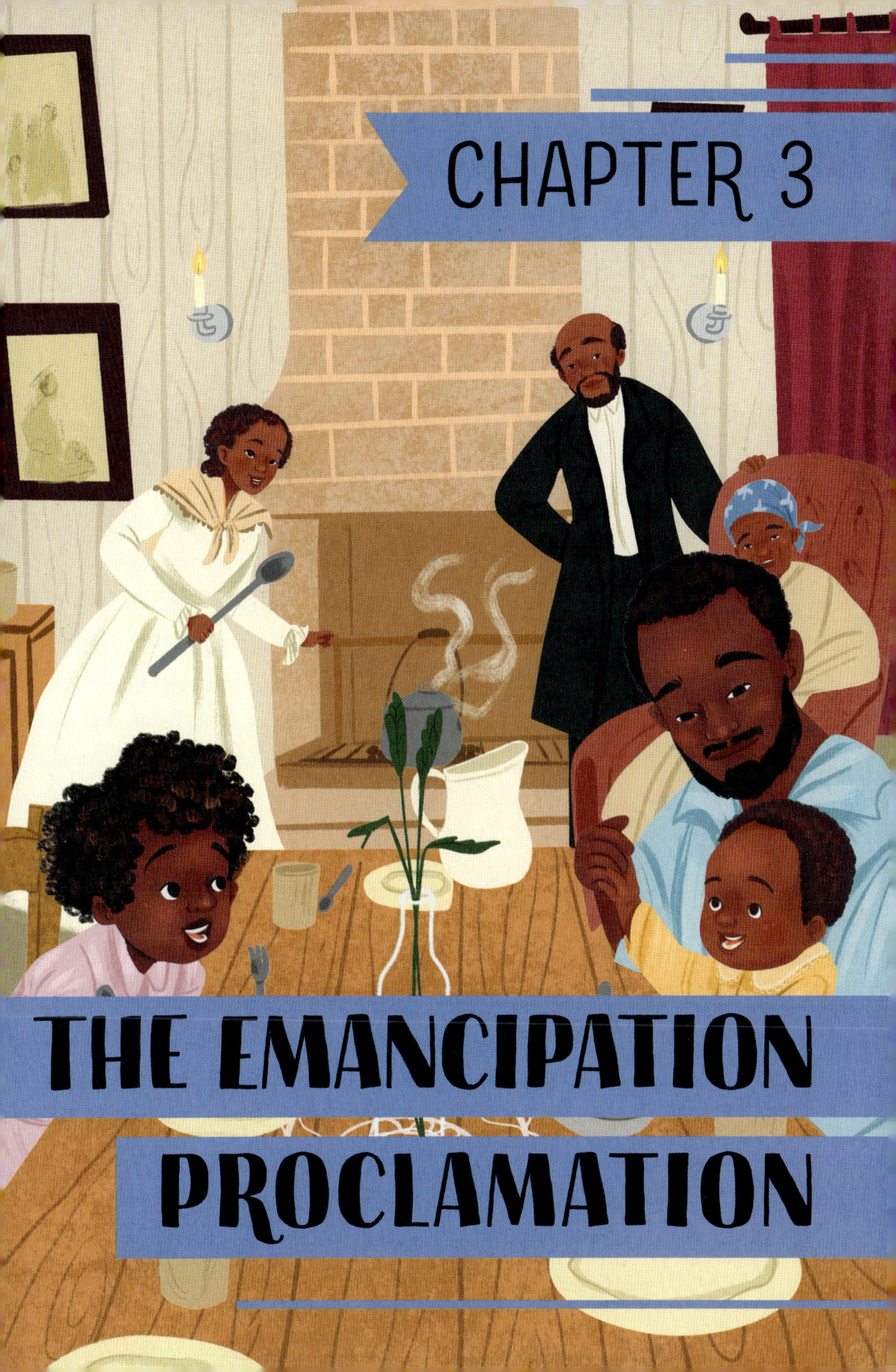

An Important Step

The Union Army struggled at first. President Abraham Lincoln knew he had to change his strategy to defeat the Confederacy. Southerners continued to use enslaved people to make money and fight the war. Lincoln began to think of ways to abolish slavery in the Confederacy. Enslaved people did not wait for his plan. When the war started, they began to seek freedom. By 1862, thousands of Black people had escaped. Many wanted not only freedom but also to fight for the Union Army. They were not allowed to fight, however, because of the color of their skin.

In 1862, Lincoln began talking about freeing enslaved people. He worried that others would not support his decision. Black leaders like Frederick Douglass urged the president to abolish slavery and allow Black men to join the Union Army. On January 1, 1863, Abraham Lincoln issued the Emancipation Proclamation. It stated that Black people in Confederate states were no longer enslaved. Across the country, people celebrated!

WHO?

Frederick Douglass was a famous politician, abolitionist, and speaker. Douglass escaped slavery at age twenty. Once free, he dedicated his life to ending slavery and speaking out against racism.

The Emancipation Proclamation did not mean all enslaved people were free immediately. Southern enslavers did not want to obey the proclamation. Enslaved people still had to escape and make it to the Union Army. Confederate soldiers and some Southerners made it very hard for them. Many people were hurt or caught as they tried to leave.

JUMP IN THE THINK TANK

Why do you think the Confederacy did not obey the Emancipation Proclamation?

Others were brought back to their enslavers and punished. But people continued to seek freedom.

The Emancipation Proclamation allowed Black men to join the Union Army. Almost 200,000 Black men signed up. Now the Union had many more soldiers to help win the war.

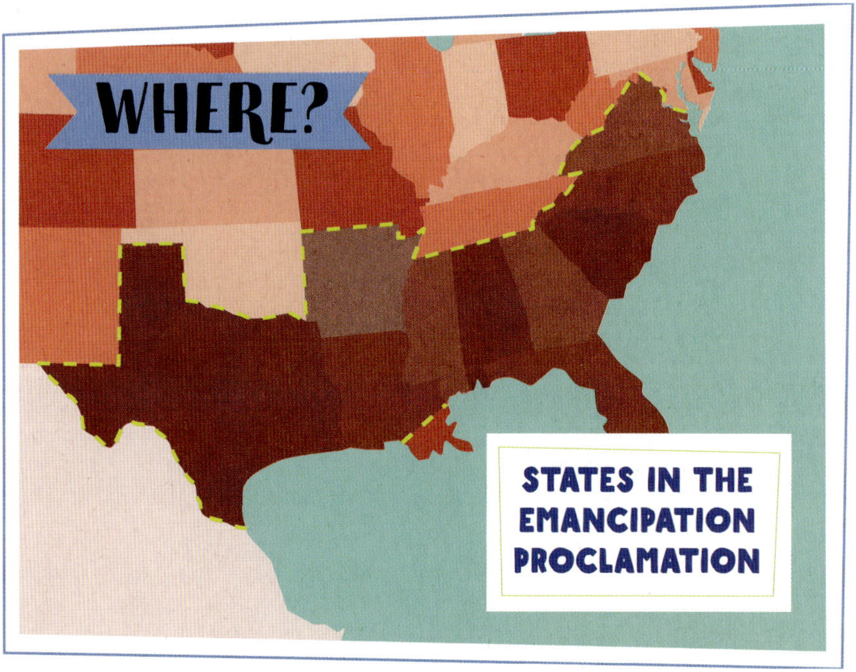

The End of the War

The Emancipation Proclamation did not immediately end the war. But it made the Union Army bigger and more powerful. The Confederacy relied on enslaved workers to farm their land, so it lost money and resources. In April 1865, the largest unit of the Confederate Army surrendered to the Union Army in Virginia. Only a few days later, President

Abraham Lincoln was **assassinated** while watching a play. Americans were shocked and sad.

As the war was ending, many Northern politicians began to fight to add the **Thirteenth Amendment** to the Constitution. The amendment would end slavery in America forever. Some politicians did not want the amendment to pass. Many people worked hard to make sure Congress approved it. On January 31, 1865,

Congress approved the Thirteenth Amendment, and slavery was declared illegal. Over the next year, Black people all over the country became free.

In the months following the war, free Black people worked to build new lives. They started paid jobs, reunited with lost family members, and continued to create successful communities. They began to start their own schools and learn. There were challenges ahead, but African Americans everywhere were excited about the future.

WHEN?

- The Civil War starts. — **1861**
- The Emancipation Proclamation is enacted. — **1863**
- The largest unit of the Confederate Army surrenders. — **1865**
- The Thirteenth Amendment is approved. — **1865**

CHAPTER 4

GENERAL ORDER NO. 3

June 19, 1865

Almost two years after the Emancipation Proclamation, more than 250,000 Black people were still enslaved. Even though the largest unit of the Confederate Army surrendered, some Confederate troops in places like Texas continued fighting the war. They believed they could still win. They refused to free African Americans and made it very difficult for them to get to the Union army.

African Americans knew they were free, but they had no one to **enforce** their freedom. Enslavers ignored the Emancipation Proclamation. They used violence to force some Black people to stay.

In 1865, Union officials knew they had to take control of the former Confederate states. They wanted to make sure Confederate soldiers stopped fighting. Union generals sent large

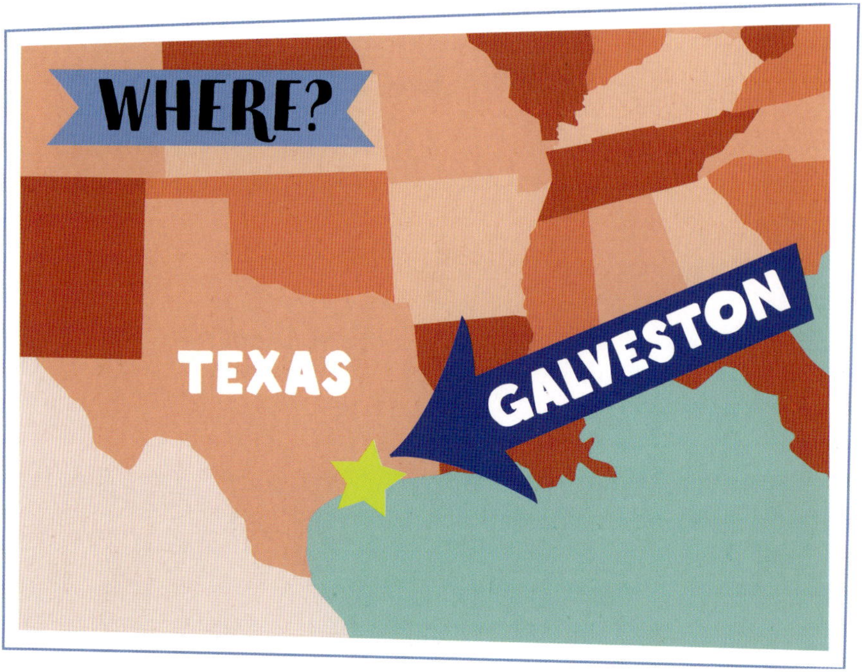

groups of soldiers to all parts of the Confederacy to enforce freedom and peace.

Union General Gordon Granger was called to travel to Texas. On June 19, Granger arrived in Galveston, Texas, with nearly 2,000 soldiers. Most of them were in the United States Colored Troops. Finally, the Union Army had arrived! General Granger read General Order No. 3. This order stated that enslaved people were free.

More important, they now had Union soldiers to protect them and to make sure they would stay free.

WHO?

The United States Colored Troops, or USCT, were groups of Black soldiers who fought for the Union Army. By the end of the war, they made up one tenth of all Union soldiers!

The First Moments of Freedom

When they heard General Order No. 3, African Americans in Galveston celebrated! General Order No. 3 asked Black people to stay in Texas and work for money, but many ignored these requests. They wanted to move and look for lost family members. Black Texans

knew their new freedom had no boundaries. Some stayed in Texas, but others relocated to places like New Orleans, Louisiana. Some people moved further west.

No matter where African Americans went, they faced hardship. Many people did not want Black people in their communities.

Some Southerners did not want to accept the end of slavery. Former Confederate soldiers attacked free Black people. When African Americans asked for payment for their work, many white people refused to pay. Politicians knew about these problems. They created an organization to make sure African Americans were protected. It was called the Freedmen's Bureau.

JUMP IN THE THINK TANK

How do you think enslaved African Americans felt when they heard they were free? How would you celebrate freedom?

After the Civil War, it became clear that ending slavery did not stop racism and hate. But free African Americans everywhere rallied together to build a new life. They created schools and new churches. They started successful businesses and farms. They voted in

elections. In the years following the war, sixteen Black members of Congress, including two Black senators, were elected.

WHEN?

The last battle of the Civil War ends.

MAY 14, 1865

General Granger reads General Order No. 3.

JUNE 19, 1865

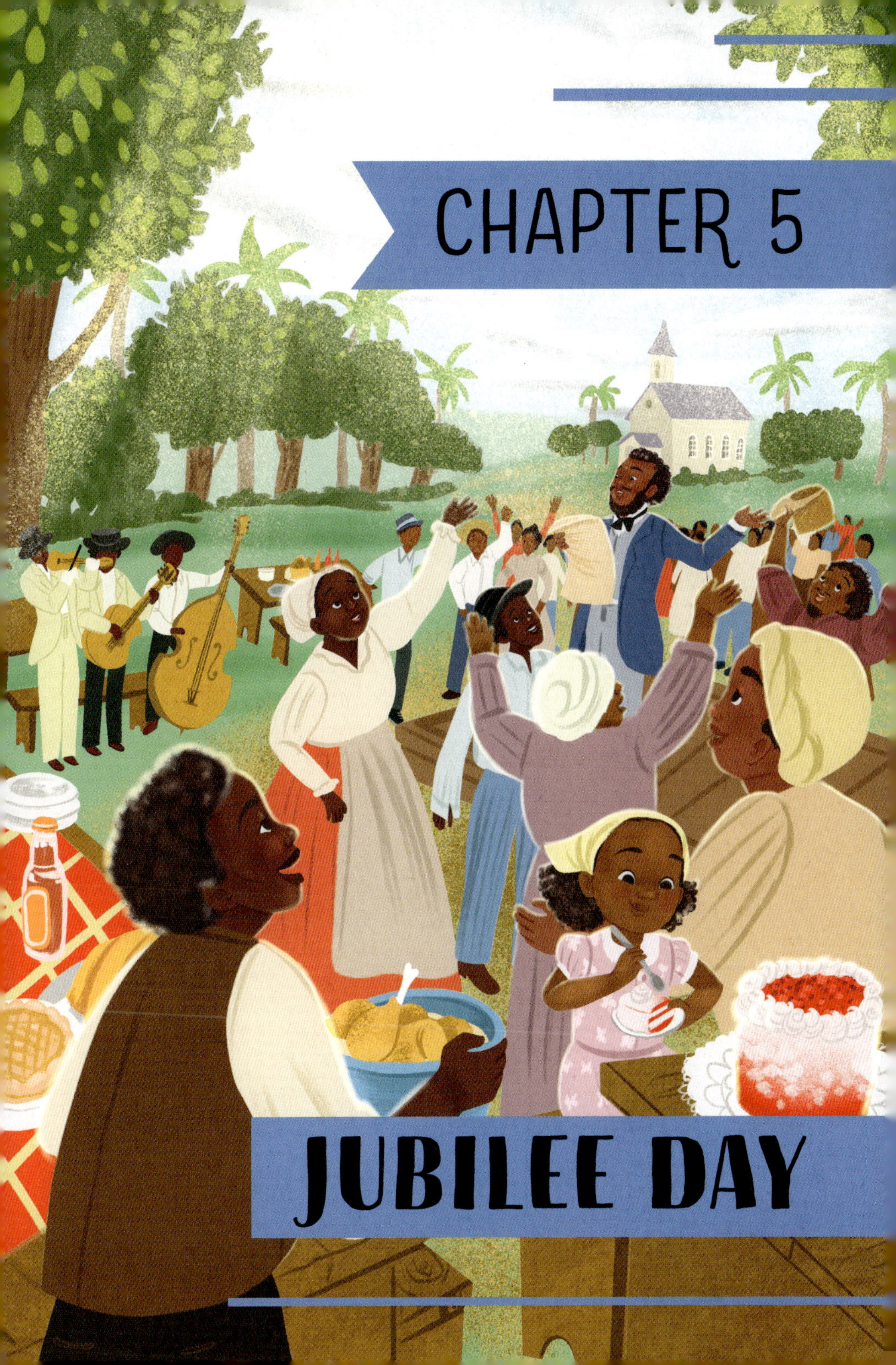

CHAPTER 5

JUBILEE DAY

JUMP –IN THE– THINK TANK

Why do you think emancipation celebrations were so important to African Americans?

Early Celebrations

African Americans decided to celebrate the day that General Granger arrived in Galveston and enforced General Order No. 3. On June 19, 1866, Black people in Galveston gathered to celebrate the first anniversary of their freedom.

At first, they called June 19 "Jubilee Day." A jubilee is a special celebration for an anniversary. The early gatherings often included food and music. People cooked traditional foods like barbecue. They also ate summer dishes like watermelon. They made a special red drink by mixing strawberries and lemonade. The red color reminded them of the suffering they had faced during slavery.

In some places, the celebrations included people reading the Emancipation Proclamation out loud. The gatherings were usually held in community spaces, like parks and churches. There were parties and parades with singers, dancers, and decorated **carriages**.

Many of the early celebrations also focused on **civic engagement**. Civic engagement is people getting together to support important causes. Black Texans wanted to celebrate freedom, but they knew freedom came with responsibilities. Even though Black people

were free, they still faced racism. Black leaders held rallies and events on Jubilee Day to support **equality** for Black people, not just freedom.

Making History

Over time, Black people started to call Jubilee Day "Juneteenth." Juneteenth is a shortened version of "June nineteenth." The celebrations continued to grow.

Black community leaders often ran into problems when they tried to celebrate Juneteenth. Even after the Thirteenth Amendment became part of the Constitution, some white Americans believed Black people were inferior. They thought Black Americans should have remained enslaved. Some white people did not want Black people to use public places for their celebrations.

In 1872, four men from the Third Ward, a Black neighborhood in Houston, Texas, had an idea. They pooled together money to buy a park to hold Juneteenth celebrations. They bought nearly ten acres and opened the park every June to honor the end of slavery. They called it Emancipation Park.

WHO?

John Henry "Jack" Yates was a freedman, reverend, and leader in Houston. He and three other men worked together to buy Emancipation Park.

African Americans came together to celebrate emancipation in many ways. Emancipation celebrations happened throughout the country at different times. Remember that enslaved people were freed at different times throughout the Civil War. Some people celebrated on January 1 because that was when the Emancipation Proclamation went into effect. Black people went to church on December 31 and waited for the clock to strike midnight. They called these gatherings "watch night services." African Americans in Richmond, Virginia, celebrated on April 3 because that was when the Union Army entered Richmond.

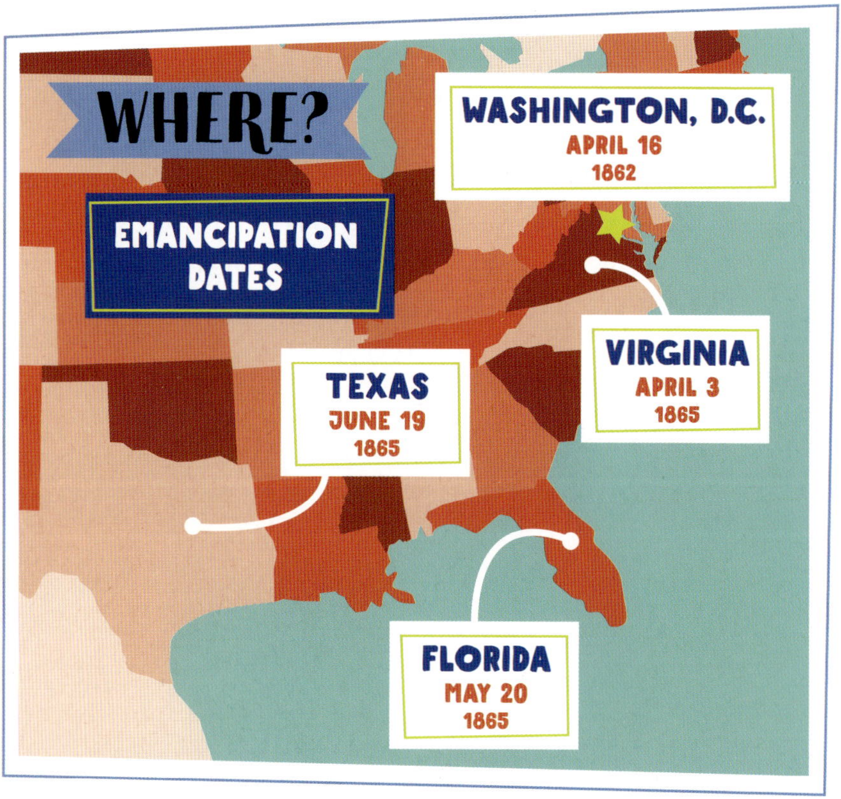

Remembering emancipation allowed African Americans to come together to reflect on their past. It also allowed them to celebrate their hard-earned freedom and to create new traditions.

The first Jubilee celebration takes place.

1866

Black leaders purchase Emancipation Park.

1872

WHEN?

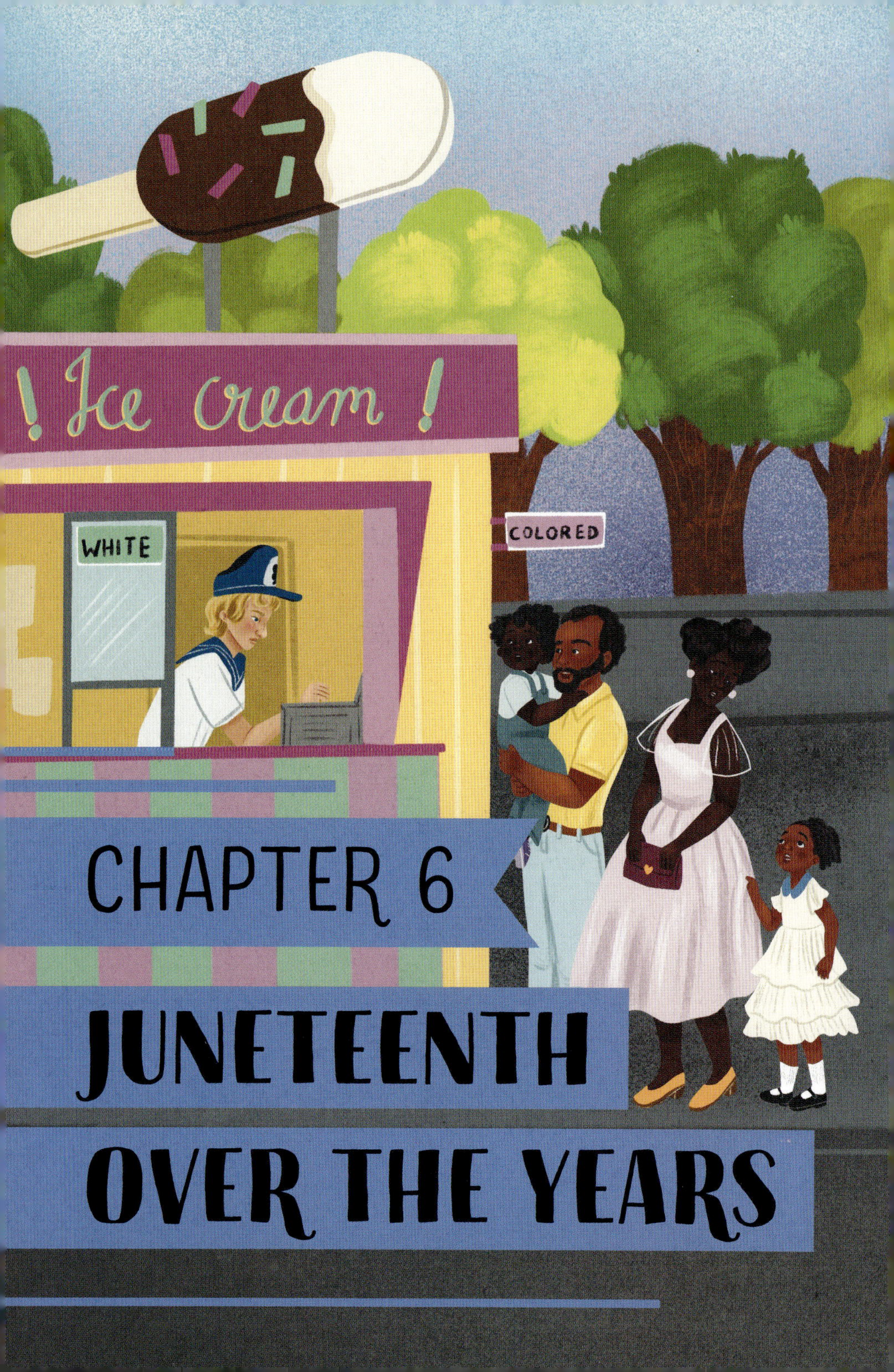

CHAPTER 6
JUNETEENTH OVER THE YEARS

New Challenges

The 20th century brought new challenges for African Americans. Southern politicians created unfair rules called Jim Crow laws. These laws kept Black and white people apart, which is known as **segregation**. Black people could not go to the same schools as white people. They were not allowed in many public places. The laws even made it hard for Black people to vote. Black people lost many of the rights they had gained after the Civil War.

Some white Southerners joined racist groups like the Ku Klux Klan (KKK). KKK members were violent toward Black Southerners who refused to follow unfair rules. Confederate supporters built statues dedicated to Confederate generals. In many places celebrating Juneteenth was dangerous.

In 1936, nearly 200,000 people showed up to celebrate Juneteenth at the Texas State Fair in Dallas. In 1938, the government of Texas proclaimed June 19 the official Emancipation Day in Texas.

This act did not stop the Jim Crow laws or the threats of violence. Jim Crow laws made holding Juneteenth celebrations difficult. But many Black people continued to organize gatherings.

WHO?

Heman Sweatt was not allowed to attend the University of Texas because he was Black. He sued the school, and in 1950 he won his case. Because of Sweatt, public universities in Texas were desegregated.

The Civil Rights Movement

From the 1940s to the 1970s, Juneteenth celebrations were overshadowed by the **civil rights movement**. In the 1960s, leaders like Dr. Martin Luther King Jr., Malcolm X, and Ella Baker created organizations and fought against inequality. They wanted fair treatment and equal rights. They organized marches and protests. Martin Luther King Jr. organized events like the March on Washington, where 250,000 people gathered to support equal rights for Black Americans.

Many groups worked together to protest segregation and fight for voting rights. They faced extreme violence. When they marched to protest unfair laws, the police often attacked them. Many protestors were put in jail.

During this time, fewer Juneteenth celebrations took place. People were focused on trying to regain the rights taken away by Jim Crow laws.

In 1968, Coretta Scott King, the widow of Dr. Martin Luther King Jr., brought attention to Juneteenth. She helped plan a protest called the Poor People's Campaign. Protestors traveled to Washington, D.C., to ask the government to help poor Americans find work and housing. King and the organizers picked June 19 as the day the campaign would end.

JUMP IN THE THINK TANK

Why do you think fewer people celebrated Juneteenth during the civil rights movement?

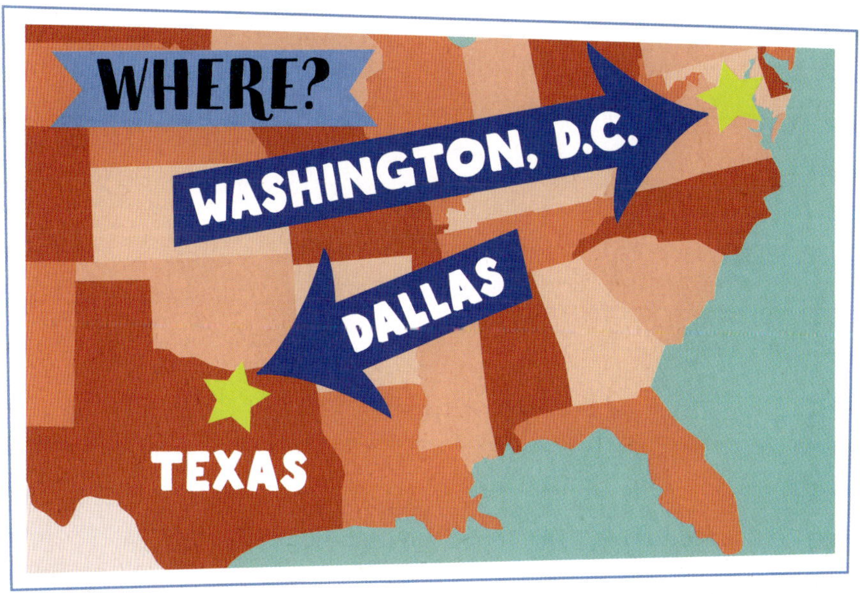

After the campaign was over, many protestors brought Juneteenth celebrations back to their own communities. The fight for equality continued, but Juneteenth was celebrated more and more.

WHEN?

1936: Juneteenth is celebrated at the Texas State Fair.

1938: Emancipation Day is made a day of observance in Texas.

1963: Martin Luther King Jr. leads the March on Washington.

1968: The Poor People's Campaign ends on Juneteenth.

CHAPTER 7

JUNETEENTH TODAY

An Official Holiday

By the 1970s, Juneteenth was celebrated in many parts of the country. Black communities honored Juneteenth and their own emancipation days. People gathered at churches, in parks, and at community centers. The celebrations included rallies for justice and equality.

Emancipation Day had been honored as a day of observance in Texas since 1938, but Juneteenth was not an official state holiday. In the 1970s, a state representative, Al Edwards, called for an amendment to make Juneteenth a

state holiday. It would mean many schools, businesses, and parts of the government would be closed on Juneteenth. Everyone would have the day off to celebrate. After a hard fight, Edwards finally succeeded. In 1980, Texas made Juneteenth a state holiday.

JUMP –IN THE– THINK TANK

If you had to create a holiday that everyone celebrated, what would it be?

In 1997, the National Juneteenth Celebration Foundation (NJCF) created a flag to be flown on the holiday. The flag includes one star representing the state of Texas and a bursting star representing freedom. The flag also includes the colors red, white, and blue. These colors are a reminder that African Americans are a part of American history.

As Juneteenth became more popular, organizers wanted it to be a federal holiday. That meant it would be honored across the nation, not just in Texas. Since 1976, Opal Lee, a well-known Texan activist, had been advocating for Juneteenth to become a federal holiday. Lee walked long distances to show her dedication to the cause. In 2021, after the hard work of people like Opal Lee and Al Edwards, President Joe Biden signed Bill 475. This bill made Juneteenth a federal holiday. Opal Lee was recognized at the signing ceremony.

WHO?

When Opal Lee was twelve, a group of white people burned down her home. This tragedy made her want to fight against racism. She is now known as the Grandmother of Juneteenth.

Celebrations Today

Today all Americans can celebrate Juneteenth. Now that it is a federal holiday, most businesses and government buildings must close for the day. Many states have begun to organize large parades or festivals. Juneteenth festivals usually include music and dancing. Local businesses decorate parade floats or serve food. In some places, people read the Emancipation Proclamation. They also sing songs and read poems by famous Black writers. Black Southerners still celebrate Juneteenth with local customs. Some people organize beauty pageants at which they crown a "Miss Juneteenth." Juneteenth is about gathering with family and friends to remember the past and celebrate the future.

Juneteenth started in Galveston, Texas, in 1865, but it is now recognized throughout the United States. For decades, Black people faced racism, discrimination, and inequality. Even when there were fewer celebrations, Black people made sure Juneteenth was remembered. They created a tradition and then worked to make sure it was honored forever.

Today we can all celebrate the history of Juneteenth and the burst of freedom that African Americans like Sarah Ashley felt in 1865.

WHEN?

1980	1997	2021
Juneteenth becomes a state holiday in Texas.	The NJCF creates the Juneteenth flag.	Juneteenth becomes a federal holiday.

CHAPTER 8

SO . . . WHAT'S THE HISTORY OF JUNETEENTH?

Challenge Accepted!

You've read the book, now test your Juneteenth knowledge by taking this quiz. The answers are on page 53, but don't peek!

1 **When is Juneteenth celebrated?**

- A. June 17
- B. June 19
- C. June 1
- D. June 30

2 **Where was Juneteenth originally celebrated?**

- A. Texas
- B. California
- C. Iowa
- D. Georgia

3 **What did the Thirteenth Amendment do?**

→ A. Made Juneteenth a federal holiday

→ B. Started the Civil War

→ C. Made Kansas a state

→ D. Made slavery illegal

4 **What was the original name for Juneteenth?**

→ A. Celebration Day

→ B. Freedom Day

→ C. Jubilee Day

→ D. June Day

5 **Why did Jack Yates buy Emancipation Park?**

→ A. He wanted to live there.

→ B. He wanted a place to freely celebrate Juneteenth.

→ C. He wanted to start a school there.

→ D. He wanted to sell it to someone else.

6 **Where was the Third Ward?**

- A. Galveston, Texas
- B. Washington, D.C.
- C. Fort Sumter, South Carolina
- D. Houston, Texas

7 **When did the Poor People's Campaign end?**

- A. June 19, 1800
- B. June 19, 1968
- C. January 10, 1965
- D. May 9, 1979

8 **What colors are on the Juneteenth flag?**

- A. Red, white, and blue
- B. Yellow and green
- C. Pink, blue, and purple
- D. Black and white

9 **Who is Opal Lee?**

- A. The leader of the Poor People's March
- B. The designer of the Juneteenth flag
- C. The activist who helped make Juneteenth a federal holiday
- D. A famous Black singer

10 **How is Juneteenth celebrated today?**

- A. With parades
- B. By singing songs
- C. By gathering with friends and family
- D. All of the above

Answers: 1. B; 2. A; 3. D; 4. C; 5. B; 6. D; 7. B; 8. A; 9. C; 10. D

Our World

Juneteenth has been celebrated for more than 150 years. As we learn about its history, we can remember the past and appreciate the changes that Black Americans have fought for.

- → Many companies and businesses give their workers the day off for Juneteenth. That gives everybody time to celebrate and remember.
- → Groups like the NAACP continue to fight for equality long after the Emancipation Proclamation and the civil rights movement. They honor Juneteenth with celebrations, but also with marches and protests for Black rights.
- → Even today, some people think that parts of Black history should not be taught in schools. Groups like the Association for the Study of African American Life and History are fighting to make sure this important history is not forgotten.
- → People continue to to honor Juneteenth with civic engagement. Many politicians are now fighting for **reparations** for African Americans. They want the government to make up for the wrong of slavery.

JUMP IN THE THINK TANK FOR MORE!

Let's think a little more about Juneteenth. How will its history inspire you?

→ Juneteenth was first celebrated by African Americans in Galveston, Texas. It was a local tradition. What are the local traditions in your town or city?

→ Learning about the way other people celebrate can teach us a lot. What is a holiday you have heard of but do not celebrate? Ask an adult to help you learn more about it at the library or online.

→ Juneteenth has been celebrated through many difficult times for African Americans. Why do you think Juneteenth has been celebrated for so long? Why is it an important event to remember, even when times are tough?

Glossary

abolished: To put an end to something, such as a law, policy, or practice

assassinated: Killed someone, usually a leader, by sudden or secret attack

carriages: Vehicles pulled by horses, which people used for travel before cars

civic engagement: People getting together to support important causes

civil rights movement: A time of struggle when Black people in the United States fought to end racial discrimination and have equal rights

Confederacy: The group formed by the Southern states that seceded during the Civil War

Congress: The part of the United States government that makes laws

continent: One of the seven large areas of land on Earth

enforce: To make people obey

enslaved: Forced to work without the freedom to choose and without pay. Enslaved people were also called slaves.

equality: When every person in a group has the same rights and opportunities

inferior: Less important or valuable

plantations: Large farms that grew mainly cotton and tobacco and that used enslaved people as forced labor

racist: Believing a person or group of people is less than another, or not worthy of the same rights as a different person or group of people, solely based on their race

reparations: Making up for wrongdoing by paying or otherwise helping people who were wronged

seceded: Left or pulled out of a group

segregation: The separation of people, usually on the basis of their race or skin color

territories: Lands that have not yet been made into official states

Thirteenth Amendment: An amendment to the U.S. Constitution that made slavery illegal

Underground Railroad: A secret network of safe houses that enslaved people used to escape slavery

Union: The Northern states that stayed together after the Southern states seceded

Bibliography

Federal Writers' Project. "Slave Narrative Project, Vol. 16, Texas, Part 1, Adams-Duhon." loc.gov/item/mesn161.

Juneteenth World Wide Celebration. "History of Juneteenth." juneteenth.com/history.

Mosley, Tonya, and Allison Hagan. "Juneteenth Food Traditions: Toni Tipton-Martin Shares Memories of Baked Beans, Devil's Food Cake."
June 18, 2021. wbur.org/hereandnow/2021/06/18/juneteenth-food-toni-tipton-martin.

National Museum of African American History and Culture. "The Historical Legacy of Watch Night." nmaahc.si.edu/explore/stories/historical-legacy-watch-night.

Texas Institute for the Preservation of History and Culture. "Juneteenth: 'The Emancipation Proclamation—Freedom Realized and Delayed.'" pvamu.edu/tiphc/research-projects/juneteenth-the-emancipation-proclamation-freedom-realized-and-delayed.

Texas State Library and Archives. "Texas Remembers Juneteenth." tsl.texas.gov/ref/abouttx/juneteenth.html.

The White House. "A Proclamation on Juneteenth Day of Observance, 2021." whitehouse.gov/briefing-room/presidential-actions/2021/06/18/a-proclamation-on-juneteenth-day-of-observance-2021.

About the Author

Arlisha Norwood is a historian, researcher, and social justice advocate. She received her PhD in history from Howard University. She has published several children's books, including *Black Heroes: A Black History Book for Kids: 51 Inspiring People from Ancient Africa to Modern-Day U.S.A*. She aims to convey her love of history through innovative and exciting methods.

About the Illustrator

Sawyer Cloud is a self-taught artist living in Madagascar, her native country. Passionate about the visual arts, she learned illustration through personal research and work experience. When not drawing, she is singing and wearing her favorite fairy costume. She lives with her family and her two pets, Arya the dog and Potter the cat. Find her at @sawyercloud01.

WHO WILL INSPIRE YOU NEXT?

EXPLORE A WORLD OF HEROES AND ROLE MODELS IN ***THE STORY OF***... BIOGRAPHY SERIES FOR NEW READERS.

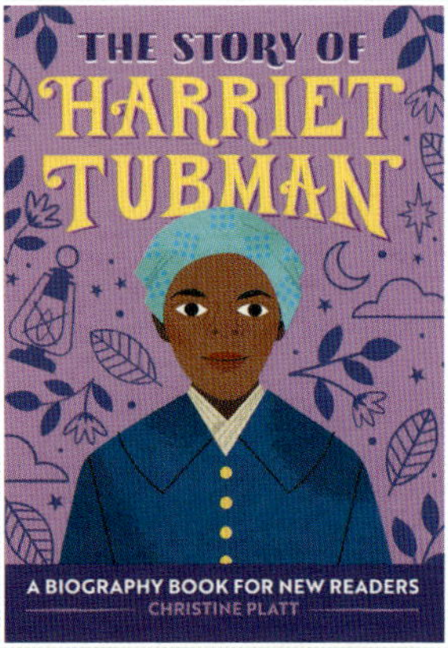

LOOK FOR THIS SERIES
WHEREVER BOOKS AND EBOOKS ARE SOLD

Alexander Hamilton
Albert Einstein
George Washington
Jane Goodall
Barack Obama
Helen Keller
Marie Curie
Simone Biles